The Mystery
—of the—
MISSING LEOPARD

Written by Alice Leonhardt

Illustrated by Erin Mauterer

STECK-VAUGHN
ELEMENTARY · SECONDARY · ADULT · LIBRARY

A Harcourt Classroom Education Company

www.steck-vaughn.com

Contents

CHAPTER 1

A New Case

Hi there, kid. I'm Clancy LaRue, the famous cat detective. Maybe you read about my last case—the missing poodle puzzle.

Miss Strake's pet poodle, Fifi, had disappeared. It didn't take a rocket scientist to figure out what had happened. Fifi had decided to go out for a walk all by herself and was picked up by the dogcatcher. She was on the way to the dog pound when I rescued her. Fifi got home safe and sound. Van doors are no match for a clever cat.

I normally don't help dogs. But Miss Strake is a friend of the family. And Fifi isn't bad for a dog, I guess. At least she doesn't have ticks and smell like old bones.

Today, however, I'm taking it easy. A morning tongue bath in a sunny spot is pure joy. But wait. Is that the sound of the can opener? Yes! I smell tuna. Breakfast is served!

With a yawn, I get up, stretch, and finish my bath. I mustn't rush to the kitchen, or Libby will think I'm easy to please. Only when my stripes are smooth and shiny do I walk into the kitchen.

Mmmm. The smell of tuna is heavenly. I lick my lips. I crouch in front of my food bowl. I open my mouth to take a bite. Then I notice the bowl is empty!

NO FOOD! I glance around the kitchen. What is going on? It's my breakfast time!

Libby comes into the kitchen. "There you are, Clancy," she says. "Did you eat your tuna already? You must be really hungry. I'll give you some more."

Hmmm. This is strange. If she put the food in my bowl, where did it go? My stomach growls.

I watch Libby open another can and spoon tuna into my bowl. "There you are. Enjoy." She ruffles the fur on my neck before leaving.

Life is good. I can chow down now. But first I have to smooth that fur she ruffled. I'm in the middle of smoothing when a noise makes me look up. The flap of my cat door is moving back and forth.

My ears prick up. Is someone coming into my house? On silent paws I sneak under the kitchen table. The cat door makes a clunking noise. Quick as a flash, an animal darts into the kitchen and RUNS TO MY FOOD BOWL!

With loud, slurping noises, the creature attacks my food. I charge from under the table. "Hey, you! That's my tuna you're stealing!"

The creature is so startled that it leaps into the air. Then it faces me. It hunches its back. When it hisses, I realize the creature is a cat—a skinny, dirty cat with a torn ear.

"And I'll bet you ate my other bowl of tuna, too," I accuse.

"So? You want to fight about it?" the cat challenges. The fur on its back bristles, but I can tell it's all a bluff. The thing's half my size and so skinny I could knock it over with one paw.

"No. You're in no shape to fight about it." I sit back and eye the creature. "But stealing is a crime, you know."

The cat's whiskers tremble. "I know, but I was starving. When I passed your house, I smelled the tuna." Licking its lips, the cat looks longingly at the bowl.

I sigh. "Oh, go ahead. You need it more than I do." It dives headfirst into the bowl and gobbles the rest of the tuna.

"What's this?" Libby asks as she comes into the kitchen. "Oh, you cute little thing!"

Cute? I look over at the cat. It runs to Libby and rubs against her leg. When she stoops to pat it, it purrs loudly.

Turning, I slink from the kitchen. I might as well face it. I'm not going to get breakfast while that thing's around.

I can still enjoy a snooze in my favorite chair. I jump up, expecting the soft cushion. I land on something hard and flat. How am I supposed to sleep on a pile of newspaper?

This day is not off to a good start, I grumble to myself. I try to nose the paper to one side. The morning headline catches my attention.

A missing cat! A feline in distress! My whiskers twitch. My tail flicks. Clancy LaRue, cat detective, is on a new case!

CITY GAZETTE NEWS

LEOPARD STOLEN
FROM CITY ZOO

CHAPTER 2
Hot on the Trail

I read the newspaper article, written by a man named Bill Gazette. It says that Midnight, the black leopard, was stolen from her cage at the zoo. The keeper's name is B.W. Brooks. He found Midnight gone when he brought her breakfast. "The thieves must have stolen the leopard during the night," Brooks told the police.

That means the thieves probably haven't gotten too far, I think. Jumping from the chair, I dash into the kitchen. Howls are coming from the sink. I smirk as I head out my cat door. Libby is giving the new cat a bath.

The zoo is several blocks from my house, but a shortcut gets me there quickly. I slide under the fence, then hurry to check out the wild cats.

The zoo isn't open yet, so it's quiet except for the sounds of animals and keepers. I pad toward the cat area, ready to check out the scene of the crime. Right away I see the empty cage.

I read the sign on the front, and I shudder. "Leopards are carnivores," it says. A carnivore is an animal that eats meat. I'm meat, I say to myself. I'll have to be very careful when I rescue my feline cousin.

Jumping into the cage, I hunt for clues. The cage is big but old. It has a pretend cave for sleeping, a log for sunbathing, and some jungle plants in a corner.

I prowl around the cage, but I find nothing strange. I stop by the open door. On the handle, I spot a red thread caught in the metal. It might be a clue! It might have come from a thief's clothing! I decide to question some of the other zoo cats. Maybe they saw who stole Midnight.

Across the walkway a HUGE white tiger is staring at me from his cage. I puff out my fur and stand straight and tall, but I'm still not much bigger than the tiger's paw.

The tiger is living in a cage just like Midnight's, only bigger. Even his food dish is bigger.

"Are you looking for Midnight?" the tiger asks when I walk closer.

"Yes," I reply. "I read in the newspaper that she was stolen."

The tiger looks at me hard and curls his lip. "She wasn't stolen," he says in a low growl.

"How do you know?" I ask.

"Why would someone steal a leopard?" the tiger scoffs. "They're not rare like me. I'm a white Bengal tiger, one of the few ever born. If thieves were going to steal a big cat, they would have stolen me."

I store this information in my brain. "That's interesting. Did you see anything suspicious around here last night?"

The tiger shakes his striped head. "Sorry. I slept like a cub."

I thank the tiger, then head to a cage on the other side of Midnight's. A margay named Kiko is sleeping in the branches of a tree. She's a little bigger than me and has spots, stripes, a long tail, and big brown eyes.

I read the sign outside Kiko's cage. Hmmm. Another rare cat that wasn't stolen. "Excuse me," I say to Kiko. "I'm a detective trying to discover what happened to Midnight. Did you happen to see anything odd last night?"

Kiko opens her eyes and yawns. "Yes, I did. I'm nocturnal. I sleep during the day, as you can see."

"Sorry to wake you up," I tell her, "but this could be a matter of life and death."

She yawns again. "Since I hunt at night, I have very sharp eyes. I saw everything last night."

"You saw everything?" I repeat excitedly. "What did the thieves look like?"

MARGAY

Kiko, a female margay. Margays live in South America and Central America. Because they are hunted for their fur, they are becoming rare.

"There were no thieves. No one stole Midnight last night," Kiko says. "You can take my word for it. I would have seen or heard something."

I thank Kiko, but she has already gone back to sleep. I walk back to Midnight's cage. I slip between the bars and think. The newspaper article said that Midnight was stolen at night. But Kiko saw nothing.

LEOPARD

Midnight, a female black leopard. Female leopards can weigh more than 75 pounds. Leopards are carnivores native to Africa and Asia. Black leopards are also called panthers.

I smell something very fishy, and it's not just the breakfast in Midnight's dish.

CHAPTER 3
More Strange Clues

I spot a man heading toward Midnight's cage, so I hide behind the sign outside it. The man is wearing a red shirt. I look at the red thread on the handle of Midnight's cage. Did this man steal Midnight? Did he leave the thread?

When the man gets closer, I see he has a name tag. "B.W. Brooks, Cat Keeper," it says. This is the man who reported Midnight stolen.

Brooks closes the cage door, then leaves. His shirt is definitely the same color as the thread. It looks like the thieves didn't leave the clue—Brooks did.

I sigh. This case is going nowhere.

Or is it? I pace along the front of Midnight's cage, thinking.

Kiko said Midnight wasn't stolen at night. But Brooks said that he discovered the leopard was gone when he went to feed her at breakfast. Very fishy, I think. Fishy!!

I leap back into the cage and run over to Midnight's dish. There's a bunch of fish heads in it. I sniff them. They're fresh.

Someone had fed Midnight breakfast. But who? Brooks told the police that when he went to feed her, she was gone! If she was gone, why would he put food in her dish?

"I saw the van streak right past me," a loud voice says.

I jump into a dark corner of Midnight's cage. Brooks is walking with two police officers. One of them is writing on a pad.

"It was a tan van," Brooks adds. "I figure the thieves put Midnight in the van and drove off. It was early morning, before the sun came up. No one's on duty at the front gate."

"We'll check for tire prints," one officer says.

"Show us where you were when the van passed you," the other officer says to Brooks.

Brooks is lying, I tell myself when they leave. If a tan van drove up to the cage, one of the cats would have noticed. But why would Brooks lie?

Suddenly a flurry of movement catches my eye. Someone is in Midnight's dish. My nose twitches. I smell a rat!

CHAPTER 4

Lion Land

I pounce, catching the furry creature's tail under my paw.

"Hey! Let go, you bully! That's my tail!" the rat squeals.

"I know it's your tail," I reply. "Why are you stealing Midnight's food?"

"I'm not stealing her food. I'm eating it. Why waste perfectly good fish heads? That's what I always say. Besides, Midnight won't be back to enjoy them."

My eyes grow wide. "How do you know she won't be back? Did you see the thieves?"

The rat gets a sly look on his pointy face. "I'll tell you what I know if you'll let go of my tail."

I think about this carefully. Never trust a rat, *I* always say. But he may have a clue that will help me find Midnight. "All right," I agree. "But no tricks."

I lift my paw. Immediately the rat dashes away. But before he disappears, he yells back over his shoulder, "The keeper left the door unlocked last night!"

Aha! So Midnight wasn't stolen! Brooks left the door unlocked, and Midnight got out. No wonder Brooks is lying. He doesn't want anyone to know he was careless. He doesn't want anyone to know it's his fault that Midnight is gone.

Now I only have to find out where Midnight went. She must have left some tracks. I jump from the cage and search the ground. At last I find a faint paw print in the mud. I put my paw inside it. The print is five times bigger than mine. It must belong to a big cat like Midnight.

I find another print and another. They lead to Lion Land, a new natural habitat the zoo just built.

I bound toward Lion Land. I see it doesn't have any cages or bars. The lion, lioness, and their two cubs live on a huge island. A moat filled with water surrounds the island. How on earth am I going to get over to the island?

I jump on top of a nearby fence and scan the area. I spy a rope stretched from the fence to the island. Do I dare? Of course I do. *Dare* is this detective's middle name!

Walking carefully, one paw in front of the other, I make it over the moat. When I jump down to the island, one of the cubs dashes over. She whacks me playfully, rolling me like a ball.

"Watch it!" I shout. I jump up and dart over to the lion, who looks at me with amusement.

"Well, little cat," the king of beasts says. "What are you doing here?"

"My name is Clancy LaRue. I'm a detective. I'm looking for Midnight."

"We saw Midnight this morning," the lioness says. "She told us she was escaping from the zoo."

"Why would she want to escape?" one cub asks. "It's so nice here."

The lioness sighs. "Midnight still lives in a cage," she explains to the cub. "The zoo started to build her a habitat like ours, but they ran out of money."

"She told us she didn't think the zoo would ever finish it," the lion adds. "And she was tired of waiting."

"Did you see which way she went?" I ask. Sharp cub teeth crunch my tail. "Ow!"

"That way." The lioness looks at the tall iron fence enclosing the zoo. "We warned her that the outside world was dangerous for big cats. She wouldn't listen."

"Thank you!" I run back to the rope, a cub hot on my tail. Before he can take another crunch, I leap on the rope. As I walk along, it sways dangerously. The zoo is open now, and a group of children squeal and giggle.

When I reach the end of the rope, another group of kids try to grab me. I narrowly escape their sticky fingers. If it's this dangerous for cats *inside* the zoo, what is it like for Midnight on the outside? I have to find her before something terrible happens!

I look for more leopard tracks. They lead to the iron fence and a tree. I look up. How did Midnight get over the fence?

I hear noisy chattering overhead in a nearby tree. Squirrels dart back and forth, squealing "Another cat! Run for your lives!"

Another cat? Had Midnight climbed the tree? Leopards are strong climbers. In the wild, they'll even drag their food into a tree.

I climb the trunk. In the fork of two branches, I see long scratches where an animal sharpened its claws. I run along a branch that hangs over the fence and outside the zoo. The twigs at the end of the branch are broken. It looks as if a heavy animal made its way to the end, then jumped.

I land in the soft dirt on the other side of the zoo fence. It doesn't take me long to find another paw print. Once again I'm hot on the trail of the missing leopard.

The leopard tracks wind through a wooded area. I hear the whoosh of cars. A busy road is up ahead. I worry. Did Midnight cross the road? Is she all right?

I hurry toward the road. A round drainpipe catches my eye. It's big enough for a large cat to crawl into.

I trot down toward the pipe. When I reach the entrance, I blink. It's very dark. It takes a few minutes for my eyes to get used to the blackness.

A rumbling growl freezes me in my tracks. Two glowing eyes stare at me. A roar rings through the pipe. In the dim light, I see the gleam of big sharp teeth.

CHAPTER 5
A Narrow Escape

"Midnight?" I ask, trying to keep my voice from trembling with fear. "Is that you?"

"Who wants to know?" Midnight roars.

"Me," I squeak like a mouse. "Clancy LaRue, detective. I read about you in the paper. It said you had been stolen. But I know what really happened. You escaped to find freedom."

She growls, and the sound makes my fur stand on end.

"Did you find freedom?" I ask.

"Yes. And it's not so great," Midnight replies. "I've been hiding in this drainpipe for hours. I'm wet and hungry."

"Why don't you go back to the zoo?"

"No!" Her roar thunders off the walls of the pipe. "Not until my new habitat is finished. And I want Jennifer to come back, too."

"Who's Jennifer?" I ask when my ears stop ringing.

"My old keeper. All of us cats loved her. She wanted the zoo to finish our new habitats. Every day she asked the zoo people about them. Every day the zoo people said they didn't have the money. They got tired of her questions. They transferred her to the zoo gift shop, and she quit."

As I listen to Midnight's story, I wonder how I can help her. She can't stay in a drainpipe forever. How can I get the zoo to finish Midnight's habitat and hire Jennifer back?

"Midnight, do you know where Jennifer lives?" I ask.

"Sure. It's 222 Leopard Lane. She used to make jokes about it. Why do you ask?"

"Because you need help. I think Jennifer is our best chance."

Midnight nods eagerly. "Yes." She leaps up. "Let's go!"

"Whoa there, big cat," I tell her. "We need to stay here until dark. We don't want anyone to see you. We don't want you to get captured before we find Jennifer."

Midnight agrees. We settle in the drainpipe and take a catnap. When it gets dark, I peer outside. I can still hear the rush of traffic on the road, but the woods are dark.

"Follow me," I say to Midnight. I creep from the drainpipe with her right behind me. When I glance over my shoulder, I gasp. Midnight is huge, with shiny black fur and paws like dinner plates. It's going to be a trick getting her to Jennifer's house without anyone seeing us.

Fortunately, I know the city well. We travel through dark alleys. Midnight's black coat helps her hide in the shadows.

CHAPTER 6

A Wild Plan

We get to Leopard Lane, and we're almost to Jennifer's house. Then a van roars around the corner. We hide behind a bush. The van's brakes squeal. It backs up. B.W. Brooks stares out the open window. His eyes widen, and then he grins nastily. "He sees us! Run!" I shout to Midnight. "We have to get to Jennifer's house before Brooks catches us!"

Midnight takes off across the lawn. Her stride is so long that she reaches Jennifer's front porch way ahead of me. She leaps up, her paws hitting the doorbell.

As I gallop after her, I hear the van racing toward us. Brooks turns into the driveway.

I jump for the porch steps just as the door opens. A young woman looks out. Her eyes widen in amazement.

"Midnight?" the young woman asks.

We don't have time to hang around outside. Midnight lunges past her and into the house. As I dart around her legs, I hear the van door slam.

"Hey! That's my leopard!" Brooks yells.

Midnight ducks out of sight behind the sofa. I hide behind a chair, then peek around it. My paws get sweaty. Will Jennifer turn Midnight over to Brooks?

"I thought it was the zoo's leopard," Jennifer says coolly. "And I thought she'd been stolen!"

"Well, um . . . uh . . . ," I hear Brooks stammer. "She must have gotten away from the thieves."

"I don't think so," Jennifer says. "But I think you know what happened."

"And I think you'd better give me that dangerous animal before she eats you," Brooks warns Jennifer.

"Midnight has never been dangerous," Jennifer says angrily. "It's time for you to leave, Buster."

"I'll leave," Brooks says flatly. "But I'll be back. And I'll bring the police with me!" A few seconds later, I hear the van start up. When Jennifer closes the door, I sigh with relief.

Midnight comes out from behind the sofa and rubs against Jennifer. Jennifer pats the leopard's head. "I missed you, too, Midnight! And who is this?" she asks when she sees me.

Clancy LaRue, detective, I want to tell her, but I don't know how to talk to humans. Neither does Midnight.

"Why did you run away?" Jennifer asks Midnight.

How do I tell her that Midnight wants a new habitat? I prowl around the living room, looking for something to help me explain. On Jennifer's desk I spy a zoo brochure. It has a picture of Lion Land on the front.

Grabbing the brochure in my teeth, I carry it over and drop it at Jennifer's feet. I tap the picture with my paw. Then I look up at Midnight.

Jennifer's brow wrinkles. Her eyes go from the brochure to Midnight. "I think I understand," she finally says to Midnight. "You don't want to live in a cage anymore."

Midnight makes a noise like a leopard meow. She looks at Jennifer with sad eyes.

Jennifer scratches Midnight's neck. "Okay, Midnight," she says in a firm voice. "It's time for some action." She jumps to her feet and grabs the phone. She dials and asks for Bill Gazette, the reporter from the newspaper. She tells him everything. "Get them over here right away!" she says. When Jennifer hangs up, there's a big smile on her face. "Midnight, I think your problem will soon be solved!"

I punch my paw in the air. YES!

"Let's celebrate," Jennifer says and heads for the kitchen. "Hamburger, anyone?"

She cooks up a hamburger the size of a football. I take a few dainty bites, and Midnight gulps the rest. Then she sits in the living room and cleans her giant paws.

When the doorbell rings, Jennifer opens the door. A group of people are standing on the porch. B.W. Brooks is one of them. "Come in," Jennifer says to them. Midnight glides behind the sofa.

They file slowly in, tiptoeing around Midnight. I recognize the two police detectives. I'm not sure who the others are. I figure they have something to do with the zoo.

Jennifer clears her throat, and everyone gets quiet. "I asked you to come here so I could tell you the truth about Midnight," Jennifer says. "She was not stolen."

Jennifer frowns at Brooks. "Midnight ran away. Someone must have left her cage door unlocked.

"Many of you belong to the Friends of the Zoo," Jennifer went on. "You know that the zoo has stopped work on the new living areas. Midnight ran away because the zoo stopped working on her new habitat."

"Midnight told you that? Ha!" Brooks scoffs. "Cats don't talk. Besides, who'd believe a dumb animal anyway?"

The ladies and men from the Friends of the Zoo shoot Brooks a nasty look. I guess they like animals as much as Jennifer does. Then one of the police detectives says, "Actually, Brooks, we've done some checking. We're pretty sure there were no thieves. Seems you have some explaining to do. You need to come down to the police station with us."

"But what about that leopard?" Brooks protests. "That animal is dangerous. Aren't you going to take her in, too?"

Everybody looks down at Midnight, who's now stretched out by the fireplace, fast asleep.

"I think Midnight is in good hands," one of the officers says before they hustle Brooks out the door.

"Let's get this straight, Jennifer," a man says after they leave. He's holding a pencil and pad, so I figure he's Bill Gazette. "Midnight is miserable in her cage. She wants the zoo to finish her habitat."

"That's right. And I believe that the Friends of the Zoo—with the city's help—can raise the money for it.

"I've even come up with some ideas for raising the money," Jennifer tells Bill Gazette. She goes over to her desk and picks up a piece of paper. "First, we could ask people who come to the zoo to give money for Midnight's new home. Second, we could ask all the children in the schools to draw pictures of Midnight. We could sell the drawings at the zoo. And that's just a start."

"Perhaps a visit from Midnight will make the city council want to give money for her habitat," one man suggests.

"A bake sale!" another man called out.

"Zoo license plates!" a woman offered.

"Wild cat stickers!" said another.

"An article in the paper will be a good start," says the reporter. "I can see the headline now—'Wild Cat Gets the Best.'"

Everyone agrees that these are terrific ideas. In all the excitement, Midnight wakes up and begins to purr loudly. The Friends of the Zoo crowd around her and Jennifer.

"Jennifer, we need you back at the zoo to work with the cats," a lady says.

"Sounds good to me," Jennifer replies happily. "I've really missed Midnight and the rest of them."

I sigh with happiness. It's time to head home. The reporter is busy talking to Jennifer and Midnight. No one seems to notice me. One of the Friends of the Zoo finally opens the front door, and I sneak out into the night.

I don't need to be in tomorrow's headlines. The mystery of the missing leopard is solved. Midnight and Jennifer are happy. That's all I need.

Another case closed. Clancy LaRue, cat detective, has done it again. Tail high, I strut down the steps and into the night. My stomach is growling. That new cat at home ate all my breakfast. I hope it hasn't eaten my dinner, too.